JUMP SHOT

by David Sabino
illustrated by Charles Lehman

Ready-to-Read

SIMON SPOTLIGHT

An imprint of Simon & Schuster Children's Publishing Division
New York   London   Toronto   Sydney   New Delhi
1230 Avenue of the Americas, New York, New York 10020
This Simon Spotlight edition December 2018
Text copyright © 2018 by Simon & Schuster, Inc.
Illustrations copyright © 2018 by Simon & Schuster, Inc.

For information about special discounts for bulk purchases, please contact Simon & Schuster Special Sales at
1-866-506-1949 or business@simonandschuster.com.
Manufactured in the United States of America 1118 LAK
2 4 6 8 10 9 7 5 3 1
Cataloging-in-Publication Data for this title is available from the Library of Congress.
ISBN 978-1-5344-3245-1 (hc)
ISBN 978-1-5344-3244-4 (pbk)
ISBN 978-1-5344-3246-8 (eBook)

GLOSSARY

AIR BALL: A missed shot that doesn't touch the rim or backboard

ALLEY-OOP: A pass above the basket that a teammate catches and slam-dunks

ASSIST: A pass that leads directly to a basket

BUZZER-BEATER: A last-second shot scored right before the end of a quarter

CENTER: Typically the tallest person on the team, who is able to get close to the basket, get lots of rebounds, and block the other team from scoring

DEFENSE: Trying to keep the other team from scoring points

DRIBBLING: Bouncing the ball

FIELD GOAL: A basket made during regular play, but not a free throw

FOUL: Contact with an opponent that is against the rules

FOUL OUT: If a player commits five fouls during a game, they cannot play anymore

FREE THROW: A one-point shot made from the free-throw line that cannot be blocked (also called a "foul shot")

LAYUP: A two-point shot made very close to the basket

NATIONAL BASKETBALL ASSOCIATION (NBA): The organization that oversees professional basketball in the United States of America

OFFENSE: When the team with the ball is trying to score points

(THE) PAINT: The area between the free-throw line and the basket

PASSING: When a player throws the ball to a teammate

POINT GUARD: Typically the fastest team member, who leads the offense by dribbling the ball and passing to teammates to shoot

POWER FORWARD: Team member who plays close to the basket and is known for their strength and ability to get rebounds

REBOUND: Grabbing the ball after a shot is missed

SHOOTING GUARD: Usually the best team member at jump shots and who helps the point guard set up a play

SLAM DUNK: Throwing the ball hard into the basket from above

SMALL FORWARD: The most adaptable player on the team, who is good at scoring close to the basket and from far away

STEAL: Taking the ball away from the other team before they get a chance to shoot

SWISH: A shot that goes through the basket but only hits the net (it makes a swish sound!)

THREE-POINTER: A long shot taken from behind a special line that is worth three points

TRAVELING: Walking without bouncing the ball

Hi there! My name is Jeremy,
and I'm a basketball referee.
My job is to make sure the game
is fair and everyone plays by
the rules.
I'm heading to the championship
game between the Tigers and
the Sharks.
Want to come along?

Basketball is one of the most popular and exciting sports in the world. More than one billion people watch and play basketball in nearly every country.

People have been playing basketball
for more than 120 years.
It was invented by James Naismith.
He was a coach in charge of a class
of young boys.
He noticed they were very restless
during the winter when they could
not play outside.
So he invented a game
they could play indoors.

In the first game ever,
players tried to score by throwing
a ball into peach baskets
hung from a high railing.
Every time a player scored,
someone had to climb a ladder
to get the ball out!

SPRINGFIELD, MASSACHUSETTS
DECEMBER 21, 1891

This is where the Tigers play.
I enter a special door just like
the players, coaches, and mascots.

Let's go into the Sharks' locker room
to say hello!
The coach is reviewing plays
with some players.
He writes on the whiteboard.

The *X*s represent the Sharks
and the *O*s represent the Tigers.
The trainers wrap tape around
players' ankles and wrists for support.
They also help players stretch
their muscles.

Caleb and Malik are
top scorers for the Sharks.
They are watching videos
of the Tigers' games.
They study their opponents'
strengths and weaknesses.

Other players listen to music
and relax.
Everyone gets ready
in their own way.

Now let's walk out to the court.
I stop by the scorers' table.
It is very long and a lot of people
work there during the game.
The scorers keep a record of the
different plays that happen
during the game.

They also count the points
each team scores and
add them to the scoreboard.
The timekeeper sits with the
scorers and helps the players know
how much time they have left
to play.

The announcer sits there too.
He is testing the microphone
and speaker systems.
He will tell the fans in the arena
what is happening during the game.

The television crew sits
next to the scorers.
They will film and announce
the game on live television so fans at
home can watch the game as it happens.

There was a concert at the arena last night, so the floor crew has been very busy getting the court ready. The floor is made of different pieces of wood, which they place down and fit together like a puzzle.
They make sure both baskets are ten feet high.

They also make sure that
the painted lines are
in the correct places.
These lines mark the different areas
of the court and show the players
where they can stand and where
they can take a shot.

The free-throw line is fifteen feet
away from the basket's rim.
The three-point line on the side of
the arc is exactly twenty-two feet,
but the distance to the farthest
point on the arc is twenty-three feet,
nine inches.
These measurements are used
in all NBA games.
The crew says that the court
is ready to go!

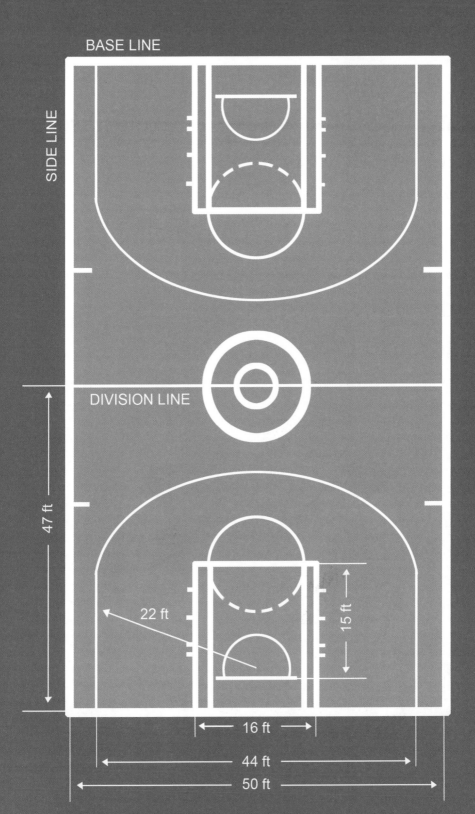

BASE LINE

SIDE LINE

DIVISION LINE

47 ft

22 ft

15 ft

16 ft

44 ft

50 ft

23

Both teams are warming up
on the court.
The Sharks focus on practice drills.
They are dribbling, passing, and
shooting layups.
Players have to keep bouncing
the ball as they move
around the court.
They also practice passing.

Layups are shots players score
when they run and shoot
close to the basket.
Malik and Caleb practice together.

They are shooting baskets.
Regular baskets are made inside
the three-point line and
are worth two
points.

Sometimes during regular play,
I have to call a foul
when a player breaks a rule.
Some examples are running into
an opponent who is trying to score,
or reaching for a ball and bumping
into an opponent.

When that happens the player
who is fouled takes a free throw.
No one can try to block free throws.
Free throws that go in the basket are
worth one point each.

Next I meet the other referees
in the locker room.
I am the crew chief for this game.
We are ready to go!

The game starts once
the players are announced
and the national anthem is sung.
Each team sends five players
onto the court.

One player from each team
stands with me
at the center circle.
This part of the game is called
the tip-off.
I throw the ball up in the air, and
they both jump for the ball, but
the Tigers player jumps higher.
He tips the ball to a teammate.

He dribbles up the court
and passes the ball to
another Tigers player.
Then one of the Sharks steals
the ball during the pass.
It's Caleb!

He runs down to the Tigers' basket
and passes to Malik.
Malik runs and stops just outside
the three-point line.
He takes a jump shot and scores.
Game on!

You don't have to go to an arena to know what happens at a basketball game. Lots of people all over the world listen to basketball games on the radio or watch on television. You can read about basketball in newspapers and on websites. You can also play basketball with your friends and have lots of fun! Keep reading to learn some fun facts every serious basketball fan should know.

TEN COOL FACTS ABOUT BASKETBALL

1. The best players in the world become members of the Basketball Hall of Fame. It is located in Springfield, Massachusetts, where the first game was played in 1891.

2. In that first game of basketball, only one basket was scored!

3. The first NBA game wasn't played in the United States. It was played in Toronto, Canada.

4. Twenty-six of the thirty current NBA teams have mascots, including Benny the Bull in Chicago, Stuff the Magic Dragon in Orlando, and Hugo the Hornet in Charlotte. The only teams that have never had a mascot are the Lakers and the Knicks.

5. Lisa Leslie once scored 101 points in one half of a game when she was in high school. The other team quit at halftime because they were losing so badly.

6. Bill Russell played thirteen years with the Boston Celtics. His team won eleven NBA championships.

7. The University of Connecticut women's basketball team won 111 straight games. The streak started in 2014 and ended in 2017.

8. The chances of winning a lottery in two straight weeks, buying one ticket each time, are better than the chances of correctly picking the outcome of every game in the NCAA Men's Basketball Tournament.

9. Michael Jordan didn't make his high school varsity team in North Carolina until his third year. Many people consider him the greatest basketball player ever.

10. LeBron James and Stephen Curry were born in the same hospital in Akron, Ohio!

EVEN MORE FACTS!

1. The USA women's national team player Teresa Edwards has won five Olympic basketball medals, the most by any man or woman in history. She won gold in 1984, 1988, 1996, and 2000, and bronze in 1992.

2. The most points scored in a single game by two teams in NBA history is 370. The Detroit Pistons defeated the Denver Nuggets 186–184 on December 13, 1983.

3. Wilt Chamberlain once scored one hundred points in an NBA game. Nobody else has scored more than eighty-one points in a single NBA game.

4. The shortest and tallest players in NBA history played for the same team. Muggsy Bogues, was five feet, three inches tall, and Manute Bol was seven feet, seven inches tall. They both played for the 1987–88 Washington Bullets.